JUICE IT!

JUICE IT!

ENERGIZING BLENDS *for* TODAY'S JUICERS

Robin Asbell

Photographs by Antonis Achilleos

CHRONICLE BOOKS
SAN FRANCISCO

Library of Congress Cataloging-in-Publication Data:

Asbell, Robin.
  Juice it! : energizing blends for today's juicers / Robin Asbell ; photographs by Antonis Achilleos.
    pages cm
  ISBN 978-1-4521-2539-8
  1. Juicers. 2. Fruit juices. 3. Vegetable juices. I. Title.
  TX840.J84A83 2014
  641.87'5--dc23
                        2013026595

Manufactured in China

Designed by Sarah Higgins
Typesetting by Maureen Forys

Prop styling by Paola Andrea
Food styling by Adrienne Anderson
The photographer wishes to thank: Adrienne Anderson for the amazing food styling, and Paola Andrea, the
prop stylist, for the myriad glasses she brought so we could choose the perfect ones for this fun book. It was
such a joy working on this project. Especially tasting all the amazing recipes. My favorite was Ginger Jolt.

10 9 8 7 6

Chronicle Books LLC
680 Second Street
San Francisco, California 94107
www.chroniclebooks.com

DEDICATION

I want to serve a big juicy glass of gratitude to all the talented people at Chronicle Books who edit, design, photograph, and make beautiful books happen. Thanks to photographer Antonis Achilleos, and my editor, Amy Treadwell. I am truly grateful to have been a part of this project, and have enjoyed every minute.

I want to pass another round to my husband Stan, and my parents, Larry and Marilyn Calhoun, and my sister, Rachael Calhoun. Thanks for enjoying all the samples.

A healthy juice toast to my agent, Jennifer Griffin, for all her help. I also owe a big plant-based ovation to Fran Costigan for serving me green juices, and to Kristine Vick, Jill O'Connor, and the rest of my friends who encourage and inspire me.

CONTENTS

03 RELAXING JUICES 80

04 PURE PLEASURE JUICES 104

INTRODUCTION

Why Juice?

Juicing just might change your life. Your juicer is a tool for making splendid beverages out of plants, unlocking amazing flavors and health benefits. Today, you can concoct a juice to be the most delicious thing you have ever tasted, and it will still be good for you. Tomorrow, you can make a juice with your health in mind, and it will still taste amazing. Juicing is a win-win that way.

Fresh juices can be so naturally sweet and satisfying that you don't need dessert, or they can be so invigorating that you don't need coffee. You can spoil yourself with a delicious spritzer or juice blend made with the tropical essences of mangoes and kiwis. You can head to the kitchen to head off chronic disease with a glass full of protective antioxidants, vitamins, and minerals from kale and beets. Or you can soothe a headache with celery juice, which relaxes the circulatory system in your head and helps eliminate toxins in the body.

Juices can be a nutrient-packed way to kick the soda habit or a way to lighten up after a period of overindulgence. The key to unlocking the energizing nutrients in plants is your juicer, which extracts the slow-to-digest fibers, giving you a concentrated elixir of vitamins and minerals that are essential to making your body hum at a cellular level. If you have been eating junk food or drinking alcohol, you may have deprived yourself of magnesium, crucial to metabolizing carbohydrates for energy. Thiamine is also essential to the cellular production of energy, and you can unlock both magnesium and thiamine quickly by juicing leafy greens for a shot of instantly absorbed natural energy. Add some vitamin C–rich lemon or tomato, and you aid your adrenal glands, which often become overworked by stress and need C to keep your energy balanced.

Intensely flavorful juices can be a valuable cooking ingredient, adding pure flavor to simple dishes. Vegetable soup increases its flavor dramatically with a shot of carrot or mixed veggie juice in the broth, and risotto takes on the essence of a vegetable when juice is simmered right into the grains.

Your juicer will deliver all of this and more.

Health

Want vibrant health? Boundless energy? Drinking lots and lots of colorful fruits and vegetables is the answer. The bounty of the produce section is guaranteed to shower your body with protective antioxidants, alkalize your pH, and nourish you with vitamins and minerals you need.

For example, let's look at the cucumber: Did you know that cukes are loaded with cell-protecting compounds? Flavonoids, lignans, and triterpenes are phytonutrients that your cucumber juice will provide. Research shows that these elements scavenge cell-damaging free radicals, reduce inflammation in the body, and block chemicals that cancer cells need to grow. Turn your attention to just about any of the vegetables and fruits that you will be juicing, and you will find similar stories, from the vision-protecting lutein in spinach and blueberries to the heart-healthy phenolic antioxidants in celery.

But most people don't seem to be able to eat enough of a variety of vegetables and fruits every day. Life is busy and meals are consumed on the run. Or maybe you are not that crazy about eating vegetables. Even the most health-conscious diner can get to the end of a day and forget to eat leafy greens. It happens.

But what if there was a way to make several servings of fruits and vegetables into a delicious, easy-to-consume snack that required no cooking, very little chopping, and no chewing? Well, there is a way. It's juicing, and it's an endless buffet of flavors, from a savory tomato-based cocktail to a sweet and sparkling strawberry spritzer.

That's right—with your juicer, you can drink raw, nutrient-rich vegetables and fruits quickly and easily. Instead of chewing through a plate of kale, juice it with a blend of vegetables and fruits, and drink it in a glass. What would have taken hours to digest is now absorbed in minutes, and you will feel the effects.

Instead of peeling, slicing, and boiling that healthful beet, drop it in the juicer, and *voilà*, you have a gorgeous glass of ruby-red goodness. Enjoy the earthy, sweet juice, because you are drinking vitamins A, B, and

C; potassium; magnesium; phosphorus; iron; beta-carotene; and folic acid. Don't forget boron, which is necessary for your body to make sex hormones.

You may never have considered whether the foods you eat are alkaline or acid, but with juices, it's all simple. Basically, meat, white flour, sugar, and many processed foods are acidifying when in your body. Plants, in general, are alkalizing, so they help balance and neutralize the acidic state of your own personal pH. Very fresh, raw plants also contain active enzymes and other trace chemicals that are destroyed by cooking. Your body makes some enzymes necessary for digestion, but raw food devotees believe that eating more enzymes in the form of raw vegetables and fruits is important to good health.

With your juicer, you can reduce an acre of healthy green salad to one simple drink. The act of juicing lets you eat raw and reap the benefits of all the uncooked enzymes and heat-sensitive nutrients. The only thing removed from fresh juice is fiber, which you can get plenty of from other sources in your diet, like whole grains, beans, and cooked vegetables. You can also make the spritzer juices in this book from whole, fiber-rich fruits and veggies, with the help of a high-performance blender, and then mix them with healthful liquids like mineral water, tea, coconut water, or kombucha to make them sippable.

Flavor

We all know that the "good for you" label can be a kiss of death. Forget about it—these juices are delicious. By blending a variety of fruits and vegetables in enticing combinations, these recipes will make your healthy diet a pleasure. Nothing compares to a freshly made juice extracted from ripe plants in your own kitchen.

Fruits are the original dessert; it's in our DNA to crave their natural sweetness. Long before chemists started tempting us with high-fructose corn syrup and artificial flavors, people refreshed themselves with juicy, fresh fruits. The sweet tastes in fruit entice us, and when we consume them, their healthfulness rewards us, unlike bottled sodas. Ditch "fruit-flavored" drinks; make your drinks from the real deal and juice the fruits themselves. Our palates crave the unique balance of sweet and tart that really good fruits provide, and we can play with that when we make our juices.

The sweetness of fruit is a perfect way to balance stronger flavors from hearty vegetables, too. You'll see when you try the recipes that a few apples make a green juice delectable, and the intoxicating sweetness of honeydew melon, blended with collard greens, creates a flavorful harmony.

The world is your juice bar. All the beautiful fruits and veggies that you can imagine can be made into delectable drinks. Persimmons, watermelons, mangoes, and pomegranates are the bright colors on your palette as you compose show-stopping sippables. Spinach, chiles, carrots, and kale are no longer side dishes—they are part of a symphony of flavors. Once you balance your veggies with a hit of healthy apple, pear, or honeydew, even picky kids will love the juice.

Fresh, unique juices and blends are so superior to bottled juices that they can be served as fabulous party fare. For a nonalcoholic party treat, buzz up some of the Pure Pleasure Juices in this book (pages 105 to 123). The designated driver can have the tastiest mocktail in the house.

For the cocktail enthusiast, these juices can be used to create exciting drinks with alcohol, as well. The difference between a drink made with freshly pressed juices and one made with a sugary mix is like night and day. The bonus is that you get some nourishment while you drink!

Cooking

Most of the time, you will probably drink your juice as soon as you make it. But don't relegate your juice habit to beverages only. Fresh juices are also versatile additions to your kitchen arsenal. Cooking is a great way to use up a juice that you didn't finish within twenty-four hours, so it never goes to waste. If you enjoy cooking with stocks, try replacing some or all the stock with vegetable juice. Soups and stews made with half water or stock and half vegetable juice will have a much more intense flavor and will be more nutritious. Grains cooked with part vegetable juice take on both flavor and color, so consider a carrot or beet risotto or spinach-and-tomato-infused quinoa. Juices can be used to deglaze a pan after searing a piece of chicken or fish or to glaze sautéed vegetables with a sweet coating. Your favorite tomato sauce will be even more interesting if you add a shot of carrot or green juice, to cook down with all the tomatoes.

How Food Becomes Energy

The human body is complex, made up of millions of cells, all of which have jobs to do. All those cells require energy. When you consume food, your digestive tract breaks it down and sends out molecules to the cells, where the cells' mitochondria then require certain nutrients and enzymes to extract energy. These nutrients are often depleted by the modern lifestyle, complete with stress, lack of sleep, and poor diet.

The most important nutrients that contribute to energy are the B vitamins, vitamins C and E, iron, and pantothenic acid.

THIAMINE (B_1): buckwheat sprouts, garlic, sunflower seeds, seeds, and nuts

RIBOFLAVIN (B_2): dark leafy greens, parsley, broccoli, prunes

NIACIN (B_3): brown rice, peanuts, wheat bran

BIOTIN (B_7): carrots, romaine lettuce, Swiss chard, tomatoes

FOLIC ACID (B_9): asparagus, blackberries, cabbage, kale, spinach

VITAMIN C: asparagus, broccoli, citrus fruits, cranberries, kale, mangoes, papayas, parsley, strawberries, watercress

VITAMIN E: asparagus, carrots, spinach, tomatoes, watercress

IRON: apples, blackberries, beets and greens, carrots, broccoli, cabbage, cauliflower, parsley, pineapple, strawberries, Swiss chard

PANTOTHENIC ACID: broccoli, cauliflower, kale

GETTING STARTED

Purchasing a Blender or Juicer

There are two basic appliances for juicing fruit and vegetables: high-performance blenders, which purée whole fruits and vegetables, and extracting juicers, which grind it up and separate the juice and fiber. Within those groups, there are endless choices.

High-performance blenders such as the Vitamix and Blendtec are great for making purées, sometimes referred to as "whole juices." A whole juice contains only the juice of fruit and vegetables (unlike a smoothie, which often contains yogurt for a creamier consistency). There are many options in the blender department, but look for a blender with a strong motor. A standard blender for home use is just not going to stand up to harder jobs and frequent use.

Your puréed whole juice has all the fiber of the original ingredients, so it will be thick. You can blend your juice and then strain it to take out the fiber if you prefer. In the recipes in this book, we will blend whole produce, then add in a flavorful liquid or some sparkling water for a juicier consistency.

Extracting juicers come in many forms. All have a feed tube for putting the produce in, some kind of grinding or crushing mechanism, and a filter to separate the fiber and pulp from the juice. Top-rated juicers are made by Breville, Omega, Hurom, Krups, Green Star, and Waring, among others. When selecting a juicer, try to find one that is easy to clean. Most of the moving parts should be able to go in the dishwasher, although there will be a pulp-filtering screen that is best scrubbed by hand with a little brush (it comes with the juicer). Decide how much space you have for a juicer on your counter and look for one that fits that footprint. If you have to store it someplace that is hard to get to, you probably won't use it as much.

Slow juicers, sometimes called "masticating juicers," are designed to process the juice without heating it, which is important.

Popular slow juicers include the Hurom and the Omega. You can spot a slow juicer by the juicing mechanism, which is more like an auger, turning and pulling the produce through as it crushes it. If you drop whole kale leaves into a slow juicer, the fibers coming out the other end will be as long as the leaf, rather than ground to bits. Despite the name, slow juicers put out juice at a pretty good speed, but without grinding the produce. These juicers keep the juice from oxidizing much while being processed. They also allow more fiber to come through with the juice, which many people will find desirable. The result is a higher yield; recipes in this book made with a slow juicer will yield 2 cups/480 ml or so.

Centrifugal, or high-speed, juicers are fast and efficient. High-speed juicer brands include the Jack LaLanne and the Breville. Most of the juicers on the market are based on this model. Generally, they have a metal blade that grinds the produce very quickly, which exposes the juice to more oxygen than a slow juicer does. They often have a bigger capacity feed tube, so you can drop things in whole and make large amounts of juice in minutes. Look for one with two speeds, because slower speeds work better for soft foods like mangoes and cucumbers, and higher speeds plow through carrots and beets in a snap. Because the fiber is filtered out more effectively, these juicers have a slightly lower yield, up to ¼ cup/60 ml less than a slow juicer. These juicers can be a little louder than a slow juicer. They may not be able to handle wheatgrass, so before attempting to juice it, read the manual.

The more you plan to juice, the more durable you need your juicer to be. Don't buy a cheap juicer that will break down if you use it every day. Features like a large feed tube save time, since you won't have to cut up the produce as finely. A powerful motor will speed up the process and will not stall or labor on the fibrous veggies that you want to juice. The best juicers produce pulp that is nearly dry, maximizing the amount of juice that you get for your efforts.

Planning to Juice

Invest in good health, and commit to making juice regularly. Juicing every day, or at least three times a week, will give you a chance to really feel the effects of pure plant nectars on your body and mind. You will get hooked on the incredible tastes and colors, and you'll want to make juices a part of your life.

Unless you have a huge garden, this commitment will mean planning and shopping. Flip through the recipes in this book, and jot down a shopping list for at least three juices. Set aside time in your schedule to purchase produce for your juice. If you have enough room in your fridge, you can shop for a week's worth of juice ingredients at one time. For many fruits, some time ripening on the windowsill is a good thing. If you want sweet, ripe mangoes, bananas, or pears, or ripe avocados, buy them up to a week in advance of when you want to use them. Check on them periodically, and when they are at their peak of ripeness, either juice or refrigerate them.

Once you get in the groove with juicing, all this will become automatic and easy. The ingredients for your favorite juices will become part of your regular shopping list, and you will start noticing when exciting produce comes to market.

Your First Juices

So, you are excited to start a new healthy habit and want to dive right in. Depending on your current diet, you may want to start slowly.

Begin with familiar, easy-to-digest fruits and vegetables, like apples, cucumbers, watermelon, and carrots. Drink about 1 cup/240 ml at a time and see how your system reacts.

You might want to start with simple, one-ingredient juices, like carrot or apple. Some stores sell big bags of carrots for juicing, and carrot juice devotees swear by their orange elixir. But variety is the spice of life. Mixing it up will keep juicing interesting. It's also a good strategy to make sure you are getting a whole array of nutrients by consuming a variety of plants. Each fruit or vegetable delivers a unique balance of valuable nutrients, so switch it up and cover all your bases.

Take a look through the recipes. Do you want to try an energizing juice to pep you up in the morning or get you through a tired afternoon? The magnesium, thiamine, vitamin C, and natural carbohydrates in a Green Lemonade (page 26) are perfect before a workout. Do you feel a cold coming on? Give the Sniffle Squelcher (page 78) a try; the vitamin C and immune-boosting echinacea tea will help you fight that cold. Is it time to wind down for the night? Give the Cucumber Mojito (page 105) a try; its minty-lime flavor is reminiscent of the famous cocktail, without the rum.

Juicing every day is the ideal, but you can juice as often as is convenient for you. Many people like to make juice in the morning and drink it over the course of the day. To get the full benefits of your juice, you should keep it tightly covered and chilled and drink it within twenty-four hours. Exposure to air will cause it to lose nutrients. I recommend keeping 2- and 4-cup/480- and 960-ml canning jars handy so you can transfer any juice you do not drink immediately to the smallest jar that will hold it and minimize oxidation. All the recipes in this book make about 2 cups/ 480 ml of juice, an amount that is easy to share with another person at breakfast or drink yourself as a cleansing meal.

Once you have made a few simple juices, let this book motivate you to try some vegetables and fruits you might not eat that often. Most of us eat the same foods over and over, limiting our intake to just a few kinds of veggies and fruits. Use the juicer to branch out, and juice collard greens, beets, kiwi, papaya, or other plants that you haven't had lately.

Drink juices that you enjoy. These juice recipes are blends, designed to be tasty as well as packed with plant goodness. If you try a juice with a strong-tasting veggie and you don't like it, by all means, stick to blends that are more pleasing to your taste buds. Good flavor is one of the big benefits of juicing. You will never stick to any healthful juicing plan if those juices don't taste good.

Juice cleanses have become very popular. The idea behind a cleanse is that drinking only fresh juices will give you the nutrients and energy you need, while you give your body a rest from digesting solid foods. If you opt for a cleanse, prepare by eating a very lean, plant-based diet for several days prior, so that the all-juice diet will not be a shock to your system. Giving up alcohol and caffeine is recommended as well. Plan to drink a variety of vegetable and fruit juices, with an emphasis on the green drinks. Drink about 12 cups/2.8 L of varied fresh juices a day during a cleanse so you are not starving yourself. During the cleansing period, it is common to have headaches and low energy as your body adjusts. Cleanses can be a way to get in balance after a period of overindulgence, whether for a day or two or up to a week. Devotees report greater mental clarity, better digestion, weight loss, clearer skin, and many other benefits after a cleanse.

Prep for Juicing

1. All the recipes make approximately 2 cups/480 ml of finished juice if made in

a slower juicer and 1¾ cups/420 ml in a faster one. Fruits and vegetables can vary, though, in how much juice they contain.

2. Buy organic and don't peel unless the recipe says to. The skins of cucumbers, apples, and carrots contain lots of great nutrients, so go ahead and juice them if they are not waxed or bruised. Kiwi skins are not recommended. Citrus fruits can be juiced peel and all, but the peel will make the juice bitter. My juicer clogs on tomato skins, so I strip off most of the peel with a paring knife. It's not necessary to get every bit off, just most of it. Seeds should be avoided; many of them contain unhealthful chemicals, taste bitter, and might hurt your machine.

3. Buy a vegetable brush and wash your produce well. Then cut the fruits and vegetables into pieces that will fit into the feed tube. That's all. No need to chop a stalk of celery; just feed it in and save yourself time and effort!

4. Read the manual that comes with your juicer. It's full of good information.

5. Think about the order in which you put your ingredients in the juicer. Big, juicy cucumbers, apples, and oranges should alternate with drier, more fibrous things like greens, herbs, or ginger. Always end with something juicy and soft to clear out the machine.

6. After your juice is extracted, put the pulp through a second time. Sometimes the last thing you put in the juicer needs a little help to make it all the way through, and that pulp often has just a bit more juice in it. The softer and juicier your veggie or fruit is, the more likely that you will need another pass, or even two.

7. After you transfer your finished juice to your glass or jar, run a little water through the juicer. It will make it easier to clean.

What to Do with the Leftover Pulp

There are many ways to use leftover pulp. Here are a few suggestions:

- Try the muffin recipe with carrot pulp on page 23.

- Carrot pulp can also be used to make carrot cake and other baked goods. It can even be sweetened and cooked to make a marmalade.

- The pulp of veggie juices is a magic ingredient for making stock: just simmer it with your other ingredients for a meat stock

21

or use it alone to make a simple veggie stock. If you are not making stock right away, freeze the pulp and save it up to make a big batch later. Stock is a great way to wring all the nutrients from your vegetables; simmering the pulp in water extracts vitamins and minerals as well as flavor.

- All-veggie pulps, such as carrot-beet, can be used to bind veggie burgers, croquettes, and veggie loaves.

- Meat loaf is another good place to blend in some veggie pulp and add valuable fiber.

- Veggie pulps can be slipped into spaghetti sauce, lasagna, or casseroles, where they go unnoticed. Stir some into a pasta or grain casserole, or even stove-top mac and cheese.

- Make a veggie cream cheese spread by blending pulp with softened cream cheese, or make a dip with goat cheese, sour cream, and your pulp of choice.

- Mix your veggie pulp with fresh chiles, lime juice, and cilantro, and you have a salsa.

- Raw foodists put pulp into a food dehydrator, which results in a high-fiber cracker.

- You can toss the crumbly pulp with vinaigrette and add it to salads.

- Leftover pulp also makes good compost, since it's already so finely ground.

- Pulp can be used to make facial masks. Carrot pulp is slightly antiseptic and good for keeping pimples at bay. Apple pulp is exfoliating, and cucumber is soothing and good for reducing puffiness. Mix in a little honey, or your favorite oil, with any of these, and you have a moisturizing mask. Just massage over your cleansed face and then relax for 10 minutes before removing.

COCOA PULP MUFFINS

If you are making a juice with carrots, beets, apples, or pears, you can save the pulp that your machine extrudes and make these big, fluffy muffins. If you like smaller ones, divide the batter among twelve muffin cups, instead of six. Moist and delicious, the muffins are packed with healthy fiber, to boot.

1 cup/150 g carrot pulp,
from 1 lb/455 g carrots
(or pulp from a mix of sweet veggies,
such as beets, apples, and pears)

¼ cup/60 ml canola oil

¾ cup/180 ml agave nectar or
maple syrup

¼ cup/60 ml nondairy milk,
such as almond or soy

1 tablespoon ground flaxseed

½ teaspoon vanilla extract

1 teaspoon fresh lemon juice

1 cup/120 g whole-wheat
pastry flour

½ cup/50 g unsweetened cocoa

½ teaspoon baking soda

¼ teaspoon salt

MAKES **6** BIG MUFFINS
OR 12 SMALLER ONES

Preheat the oven to 350°F/180°C. Line a six-cup muffin pan with paper liners and set aside.

In a medium bowl, mix together the carrot pulp, oil, and agave with a wooden spoon and set aside. In a small bowl, whisk together the nondairy milk and flaxseed and let stand for 10 minutes. Stir in the vanilla and lemon juice.

In a large bowl, whisk together the flour and cocoa, crushing any lumps of cocoa. Whisk in the baking soda and salt. Stir the nondairy milk mixture into the carrot pulp mixture and mix until combined. Add to the flour mixture and stir until just combined. Don't overmix.

Divide the batter between the six muffin cups and bake for 25 to 30 minutes (or divide among twelve muffin cups and bake for 15 to 20 minutes), or until a toothpick inserted in the center of a muffin comes out clean. Cool the muffins for 5 minutes in the pan, remove from the pan, and cool on a rack. Serve immediately.

01

ENERGIZING
juices

All juices are somewhat energizing, because the nutrients are so easily absorbed by the body. Think about how quickly you feel the effects of a caffeinated drink, or an alcoholic one. Well, a nutrient-rich drink can go to work in your system just as quickly. Juices are pure plant energy. Most fruits and vegetables provide some natural sugars, both simple and complex, which your body uses as fuel. To create and sustain energy, your body needs vitamin C, the B vitamins, iron, and copper. When you make the juices in this chapter, you are making nutrient-dense drinks that require no additional energy to digest. The energy that you would have needed to break down all the veggies and fruits in a cooked dish can instead be directed elsewhere.

The delicious juices in this chapter have been designed to give you a little extra kick. You may find that if you start the day with an energizing juice, you won't need coffee anymore. Green juices are famous for their energizing properties, so try one of those, such as the Green Lemonade (page 26), before you head to the gym. Some of these juices take it a step further. The Mango–Green Tea Booster (page 41) has instant energy in the form of banana and mango.

The Red Rush (page 34) and the Salsa Stinger (page 37), on the other hand, actually raise your metabolism. Both drinks contain chiles, which have been shown to increase the rate at which you burn calories.

GREEN SWEETIE

spinach · kiwi · honeydew · grape

4 cups/115 g packed spinach

2 kiwi, peeled

2 cups/280 g honeydew cubes

1 cup/125 g green grapes

MAKES ABOUT **2** CUPS
(480 ML)

If you want a green juice with a decadent flavor, try this fruity one. Kiwi and melon sweeten and mellow the leafy flavors, and they add antioxidants and vitamin C. Spinach is the mildest of the greens, but it still packs plenty of green nutrition.

Juice the spinach, kiwi, honeydew, and grapes, alternating among them. Run the pulp through again to extract as much liquid as possible. Serve immediately.

GREEN LEMONADE

cucumber · spinach · apple · lemon

1 medium cucumber

4 cups/115 g packed spinach

1 large apple, cored

½ lemon, peeled and seeded

MAKES ABOUT **2** CUPS

(480 ML)

This green juice is refreshing and balanced, with a tangy finish. Lemon juice serves two purposes: It brightens the sweet, mineral flavor of the spinach, and it adds vitamin C, which makes all that iron more absorbable.

Juice the cucumber, spinach, apple, and lemon, in that order. Run the pulp through again to extract as much liquid as possible. Serve immediately.

OH MY DARLING ROSEMARY CLEMENTINE

cucumber · rosemary · clementine

1 medium cucumber

1 heaping tablespoon fresh chopped rosemary

8 clementines, peeled

MAKES ABOUT **2** CUPS

(480 ML)

Clementines arrive in the late fall, in time for the winter celebrations. If you come across some satsuma mandarins, you can use those, too. Jazz up your morning juice with their unique tangerine flavor, enhanced by a mellow cucumber backdrop and the fragrant herbal note of rosemary. The rosemary is energizing and antiviral.

Juice the cucumber, rosemary, and clementines, in that order. Run the pulp through again to extract as much liquid as possible and to enhance the rosemary flavor. Serve immediately.

KALE-CARROT BONUS ROUND

kale stems · carrot · cucumber · lime

4 cups/200 g packed kale stems

6 medium carrots

1 medium cucumber

½ lime, peeled

MAKES ABOUT **2** CUPS

(480 ML)

I love cooking with kale, but sometimes I just want the leafy parts in my dish. That's when I save the stems for juicing. In this hearty juice, the assertive flavor of kale is balanced with sweet carrots and cucumber and a jolt of lime.

Juice the kale stems, carrots, cucumber, and lime, in that order. Run the pulp through again to extract as much liquid as possible. Serve immediately.

IMPROVISE

You hold in your hands a book full of fun recipes for juices. But there will come a day when you will look at a refrigerator full of produce and say, "Hmmm, what can I do with all this?"

Don't make the mistake I did, when I bought my first second-hand juicer, years ago. I worked in a store where I could get bruised produce for free, so I picked up whatever limp, mottled veggies I could scrounge and went home and juiced them all together. My juices were terrible. I felt like I was taking medicine.

Then, after talking to an experienced juicer, I realized that my free fruit was probably not all that nutritious anyway. After all, it had languished in the produce case to the point of spoiling. So, I bought some fresh veggies, and began creating blends to make my juices taste better, not to just use up random freebies.

That said, juice is a great use for that basket of really ripe plums that is beginning to develop a few bruises, or that firm, juicy cucumber with one soft end. Just trim away the bad parts. Sometimes the sweetest, most flavorful produce is a little bruised, so just use your judgment.

I've also planted my garden with an eye for juicing. Rows of greens, beets, carrots, and herbs will give you the absolute freshest juice—just wash and drop it in the hopper!

The thing I learned all those years ago, is that you need balance. Kale, broccoli, or peppers are kind of intense on their own, so if you juice them, you need some milder, and possibly sweeter, juice to make them palatable. Try apple, orange, cucumber, or another fruit you have on hand. Some juices taste a little flat without a shot of citrus, so keep lemons and limes handy. Taste as you go, and balance by adding more of one thing or another.

You can always blend in other liquids, like kombucha, coconut water, or brewed tea, for a different flavor, too.

GINGER JOLT

watercress · ginger · pear · grapefruit

1 cup/20 g watercress, leaves
and stems

One 2-in/5-cm piece fresh ginger

2 ripe medium pears, cored

2 small red grapefruit, peeled

MAKES ABOUT **2** CUPS

(480 ML)

Juice up with a lively sweet-tart cocktail with the peppery note of watercress. Ginger is warming and energizing, and watercress adds to the spicy lift. Creamy, sweet pears and tart grapefruits make this an intriguing blend.

Juice the watercress, ginger, pears, and grape-fruit, in that order. Run the pulp through again twice to extract as much liquid as possible. Serve immediately.

RED RUSH

beet · chard · chile · tomato

1 large beet

3 red Swiss chard leaves

1 small red chile, seeded

2 large plum (Roma) tomatoes, peeled

Pinch of salt (optional)

MAKES ABOUT **2** CUPS

(480 ML)

This ruby-red glass of goodness is a celebration of your healthy heart and circulatory system. Athletes are now drinking beets to improve their performance, since they contain nitrates, which relax and expand the veins. This tastes sweet and tangy, with a little chile kick.

Juice the beet, chard, chile, and tomatoes, in that order. Run the pulp through again to extract as much liquid as possible. Pour the mixture into a serving glass. Taste and add a little salt, if desired. Serve immediately.

SPROUTED GREEN BEET BLASTER

alfalfa · beet · apple · lemon

2½ cups/70 g packed alfalfa sprouts or wheatgrass

2 medium beets, with greens

1 large apple, cored

½ large lemon, peeled and seeded

MAKES ABOUT **2** CUPS
(480 ML)

The green-y sprouts of alfalfa give this sweet and tangy juice some kicky zing. And if your juicer can handle it, feel free to substitute wheatgrass. Sprouts are packed with anti-cancer compounds, which bathe your cells in protective chemicals. Wheatgrass is usually sold still growing in plastic packs, which you can set on your windowsill and keep, watered, for a couple of days.

Juice the alfalfa, beets with their greens, apple, and lemon, in that order. Run the pulp through again to extract as much liquid as possible. Serve immediately.

SALSA STINGER

tomato · bell pepper · jalapeño · cilantro · lime

6 large plum (Roma) tomatoes,
    peeled

½ cup/40 g chopped red bell
    pepper

1 medium jalapeño chile, seeded

½ cup/15 g packed fresh
cilantro, leaves and stems

½ lime, peeled and seeded

MAKES ABOUT **2** CUPS

(480 ML)

Feeling spicy? Lycopene- and vitamin C–rich tomatoes get a kick from jalapeño, which is a real energy booster. The cilantro, a cleansing herb, makes this juice taste like a trip to Mexico.

Juice the tomatoes, bell pepper, jalapeño, cilantro, and lime, in that order. Run the pulp through again to extract as much liquid as possible. Serve immediately.

ORANGE SUNRISE

pomegranate · carrot · orange

1 cup/140 g pomegranate seeds (arils)

2 medium carrots

3 medium oranges, peeled and seeded

MAKES ABOUT **2** CUPS

(480 ML)

Sweet-tart oranges are in perfect harmony with sweet-earthy carrots, and the burst of scarlet that explodes from the pomegranate seeds looks brilliant. This is a great starter juice for someone who likes O.J. for breakfast—it's a way to ease in carrot juice while retaining the flavor of a favorite morning beverage.

Juice the pomegranate seeds, carrots, and oranges, in that order. Run the pulp through again to extract as much liquid as possible. Serve immediately.

JUICY LIME GREEN TEA

grape · banana · lime · green tea

1 cup/125 g green grapes
(½ cup/65 g if using a blender)

1 medium banana, peeled

½ lime, peeled and seeded

1 cup/240 ml brewed green tea,
chilled

MAKES ABOUT **2** CUPS

(480 ML)

Green tea has a whole host of benefits, from preventing illness to aiding weight loss. It's also got a little caffeine for a boost, but if you avoid caffeine, use decaf.

For the juicer: Juice the grapes, banana, and lime. Pour the mixture into a serving glass, add the tea, and stir until combined. Serve immediately.

For the blender: Combine the grapes, banana, lime, and half of the tea in the blender and blend until smooth. Pour the mixture into a serving glass. Add the remaining tea to the blender, cover tightly, and process to clean out the remaining purée. Pour into a serving glass and stir to combine. Serve immediately.

MANGO-GREEN TEA BOOSTER

mango · banana · green tea

2 medium mangoes, pitted and peeled (1 if using a blender)

1 medium banana, peeled (½ banana if using a blender)

1 cup/240 ml brewed green tea, chilled

MAKES ABOUT **2** CUPS
(480 ML)

This purée of tropical mango and banana will boost your energy, and the addition of green tea enhances the effect. You can opt for decaf tea if you want and still enjoy the super antioxidants of green tea.

For the juicer: Juice the mangoes and banana, in that order. Run the pulp through three times to extract as much liquid as possible. Pour the mixture into a serving glass, add the tea, and stir until combined. Serve immediately.

For the blender: Combine the mango, ½ banana, and tea in the blender and blend until smooth. If you want a thinner drink, add a little cold water along with the other ingredients. Serve immediately.

SWEET PEA TEA

snap pea · pea shoot · grape · green tea

2 cups/170 g snap peas

2 cups/40 g pea shoots

1½ cups/190 g green grapes

1 cup/240 ml brewed green tea, chilled

MAKES ABOUT **2** CUPS

(480 ML)

Bursting with the sweet flavor of garden-fresh peas and packed with vitamins A, C, and folic acid, pea shoots are growing in popularity. You can buy them next to the sprouts in many grocery stores. The mellow flavor of snap peas gets a little sugar from the grapes and an energizing zing from the green tea.

Juice the snap peas, pea shoots, and grapes, in that order. Pour the mixture into a serving glass, add the tea, and stir until combined. Serve immediately.

02

HEALING
juices

Juicing is a great way to stay healthy. Drinking vitamin-rich juices helps ward off pesky illnesses, like colds. When your body is really fully nourished, your immune system is at its best, ready to fight the occasional bug.

Juices include a cornucopia of antioxidant and anti-inflammatory chemicals, which ward off serious illness as well. When you drink a glass of brilliantly hued, flavorful juice, you bathe your cells in the protective chemicals that prevent oxidation and premature aging. Diets high in plant foods are associated with much lower risks of cancer and other illnesses, and juices are the mother lode of all that great protective stuff.

The juices in this chapter are all geared toward feeding your body natural prevention. Some of them, like Hangover Fix (page 63) or Red Relief (page 73), harness the anti-inflammatory, pain-relieving qualities of certain plants. Others, like Pineapple Digestif (page 75), feature enzyme-rich fruits that are known to help digest food. You can even make use of herbal wisdom and drink the Mood Lifter (page 50), which contains delicious basil leaves, long known for their uplifting properties.

Juice can be a valuable tool for maintaining optimal health. And unlike pills and powders, it is tasty, too!

VEGETABLE SIX

parsley · carrot · spinach · bell pepper · celery · tomato

1 cup/30 g packed fresh parsley, leaves and stems

2 medium carrots

1 cup/30 g packed spinach

1 cup/85 g chopped red bell pepper

2 celery ribs

4 large plum (Roma) tomatoes, peeled

MAKES ABOUT 2 CUPS
(480 ML)

Veggie juice cocktails tend to be mostly tomato juice, with barely a whisper of other vegetables. In this delicious, savory drink, the tomatoes provide merely the backdrop for a harmonious blend of flavors.

Juice the parsley, carrots, spinach, bell pepper, celery, and tomatoes, alternating between the leafy and the juicy vegetables and finishing with the tomatoes. Run the pulp through again to extract as much liquid as possible. Serve immediately.

SUPER PROTECTOR

broccoli · orange · apple

2 cups/115 g chopped broccoli, stems and florets

2 large oranges, peeled and seeded

1 large apple, cored

MAKES ABOUT **2** CUPS

(480 ML)

Sip a lively glass of apple and orange juice blend, with a little broccoli thrown in for color! If you are feeling a little under the weather, this vitamin C– and antioxidant-rich juice is just the ticket, and you can hardly tell you are having broccoli.

Juice the broccoli, oranges, and apple, in that order. Run the pulp through again to extract as much liquid as possible. Serve immediately.

TUMMY TAMER

cabbage · mint · cucumber

1 cup/55 g packed chopped green cabbage

¼ cup/10 g packed fresh mint

2 medium cucumbers

MAKES ABOUT 2 CUPS

(480 ML)

This soothing, mild juice delivers a dose of stomach-soothing cabbage, with a tasty sparkle of mint. Cabbage juice is potent, so blending it with cucumber juice makes it more appealing while preserving its healthful effects.

Juice the cabbage, mint, and cucumbers, in that order. Run the pulp through again to extract as much liquid as possible. Serve immediately.

GLOWING SKIN

carrot · ginger · celery

6 **medium carrots**

One **1-in/2.5-cm piece fresh ginger**

8 **celery ribs**

MAKES ABOUT **2** CUPS

(480 ML)

Sweet carrot juice, a revered skin food, gets a little veggie snap from celery, which is very cleansing. Ginger adds both spice and anti-bacterial qualities. Expect to glow from the inside out! The pulp from this juice is perfect for the muffin recipe on page 23.

Juice the carrots, ginger, and celery, in that order. Run the pulp through again to extract as much liquid as possible. Serve immediately.

MOOD LIFTER

carrot · basil · beet

12 medium carrots

½ cup/30 g packed fresh basil,
leaves and stems

2 large beets

MAKES ABOUT **2** CUPS

(480 ML)

This sweet and cheery red juice gets its intriguing herbal flavor from basil—that familiar ingredient in pesto—which is juiced right in. Basil is often prescribed as an herbal antidepressant, and it will remind you of summer no matter what time of the year you drink it.

Juice the carrots, basil, and beets, in that order. Run the pulp through again to extract as much liquid as possible. Serve immediately.

MELON COLLIE

collard greens · apple · honeydew

5 cups/225 g packed collard
greens

1 large green apple, cored

2 cups/280 g honeydew cubes

MAKES ABOUT **2** CUPS
(480 ML)

If you want to drink your vitamins A and C—along with lots of thiamine, potassium, and niacin—juice collard greens. Green apple adds tartness, and creamy melon sweetens and cools the mix.

Juice the collard greens, apple, and honeydew, alternating among the three and ending with melon. Run the pulp through again to extract as much liquid as possible. Serve immediately.

GREEN CLEAN

collard greens · parsley · grape

4 cups/170 g packed collard greens

1 cup/30 g packed fresh parsley, leaves and stems

2½ cups/315 g green grapes

MAKES ABOUT **2** CUPS

(480 ML)

Collard greens are a traditional Southern soul food, and they are packed with vitamins A, C, and K in their deep-green leafy goodness. Here you can drink a pile of them, with sweet-tart grapes and some peppery parsley to make the juice really tasty.

Juice the collard greens, parsley, and grapes, alternating between the three. Run the pulp through again to extract as much liquid as possible. Serve immediately.

ORANGE POPPER

watercress · orange · lemon

1 cup/20 g packed watercress,
leaves and stems

5 large oranges, peeled and
seeded

½ large lemon, peeled and
seeded

MAKES ABOUT **2** CUPS
(480 ML)

Plain orange juice is fine, but it's even better ramped up with the spicy nutritiousness of watercress, which is rich in folate, pantothenic acid, copper, and vitamins A, C, and E. Adding a splash of lemon balances and adds more C. When you see fun varieties of orange, like Cara Cara, use them in this juice for a change of pace.

Juice the watercress and oranges, alternating between the two. Juice the lemon. Run the pulp through again to extract as much liquid as possible. Serve immediately.

KALE COUNTRY

kale · carrot · beet

1 big bunch kale, leaves and stems

2 medium carrots

2 small beets

MAKES ABOUT **2** CUPS
(480 ML)

I love making this juice. An entire bunch of kale melds with sweet, iron-rich root vegetables for a tasty treat. Earthy and mineral-y, this juice floods your body with vitamins A and C and a healthy dose of calcium.

Juice the kale and carrots, alternating between the two. Juice the beets. Run the pulp through again to extract as much liquid as possible. Serve immediately.

JUICING KALE

Kale, a member of the cabbage family, has gone from obscurity to stardom. The leafy green has been discovered by chefs, healthy eaters, and juicers, who embrace its green goodness.

A big driver of this newfound popularity is the fact that kale contains so many nutrients that protect the body. One cup of pure kale juice (including leaves and stems) has 194% of the vitamin A, 302% of the vitamin C, 31% of the calcium, and 50% of the iron needed for your whole day. Vitamin B_6, copper, vitamin K, and folate all make good showings in kale. These are potent anti-cancer, anti-inflammatory, pro-wellness nutrients.

Kale juice is something of an acquired taste, which is why it's usually mixed with other juices. Don't be put off by the idea of drinking kale. Once you mix in some sweet apples or melons, you will hardly know it's there.

Although your juicer will make quick work of bundles of kale, it is so full of fiber that it yields a surprisingly small amount of liquid. A great way to maximize its benefits is to save any kale stems you trim off when you use kale in another recipe. Just be sure to juice them within a day or two.

Try juicing other greens, from collard greens to spinach, and see which you like the best!

TART 'N' GREEN

spinach · carrot · cucumber · lime

4 cups/115 g packed spinach

2 medium carrots

2 small cucumbers

½ lime, peeled

MAKES ABOUT **2** CUPS

(480 ML)

If kale sounds a little too intense to you today, try this mild, spinach-infused drink, mellowed with cucumber and spiked with lime. Spinach is full of iron, and since you can optimize the absorption of it with vitamin C, the lime will facilitate that nicely.

Juice the spinach, carrots, cucumbers, and lime, alternating between the four. Run the pulp through again to extract as much liquid as possible. Serve immediately.

BIG SALAD

romaine · tomato · celery · lemon

1 head romaine lettuce

4 medium plum (Roma) tomatoes, peeled

2 celery ribs

½ large lemon, peeled and seeded

MAKES ABOUT **2** CUPS

(480 ML)

All the flavors you love in a salad are in this deeply flavored juice. The natural juiciness and slightly salty flavor of lettuce combine with tangy tomatoes, celery, and lemon for a veggie flavor blast.

Juice the romaine, tomatoes, celery, and lemon, in that order. Run the pulp through again to extract as much liquid as possible. Serve immediately.

LEAN GREEN

celery · parsley · cucumber

4 celery ribs

¾ cup/20 g packed fresh
parsley, leaves and stems

1 medium cucumber

MAKES ABOUT **2** CUPS
(480 ML)

Cleanse your system and suppress your appetite with this sprightly green juice. With cooling cucumber and peppery parsley, it's not sweet. Cucumber is alkalizing, reduces water retention, and helps balance blood sugar.

Juice the celery, parsley, and cucumber, in that order. Run the pulp through again to extract as much liquid as possible. Serve immediately.

HANGOVER FIX

celery · spinach · orange

11 celery ribs

4 cups/115 g packed spinach

3 large oranges, peeled and
seeded

MAKES ABOUT **2** CUPS
(480 ML)

Celery relaxes the circulatory system in your head, so it's a great hangover remedy. The magnesium in spinach also relieves a head-ache, and oranges boost your vitamin C.

Juice the celery, spinach, and oranges, in that order. Run the pulp through again to extract as much liquid as possible. Serve immediately.

CLEAR HEAD

celery · radish · garlic · tomato

4 celery ribs

2 radishes

1 garlic clove

2 medium plum (Roma) tomatoes, peeled

MAKES ABOUT **2** CUPS

(480 ML)

The snappy spiciness of radishes perks up this tomatoey concoction, clearing your head while feeding your immune system. A clove of garlic helps fight colds, and it tastes great, too.

Juice the celery, radishes, garlic, and tomatoes, in that order. Run the pulp through again to extract as much liquid as possible. Serve immediately.

BRIGHT EYES

blueberry · plum · carrot

1 cup/170 g blueberries

2 medium plums, pitted

6 medium carrots

MAKES ABOUT  2 CUPS

(480 ML)

The bright blue berries and purple plums give this drink a sweet shade of violet, and the sweet-tart fruit balances the sweet, earthy carrots. Blueberries and carrots are famously good for your eyes.

Juice the blueberries, plums, and carrots, in that order. Run the pulp through again to extract as much liquid as possible. Serve immediately.

65

HEALING
JUICES

CRANBERRY COCKTAIL

cranberry · ginger · orange · apple

2 cups/225 g cranberries

One 1-in/2.5-cm piece fresh ginger

2 large oranges, peeled and seeded

1 large apple, cored

MAKES ABOUT **2** CUPS

(480 ML)

Don't buy that sugary cranberry drink! Make your own from tangy, antioxidant- and vitamin C–rich cranberries, sweetened with oranges and an apple. Ginger gives the drink a holiday feel.

Juice the cranberries, ginger, oranges, and apple, in that order. Run the pulp through again to extract as much liquid as possible. Serve immediately.

SKINNY HOT LEMONADE

lemon · apple · jalapeño

1 large lemon, peeled and seeded

2 large apples, cored

1 to 2 jalapeño chiles, seeded

MAKES ABOUT **2** CUPS

(480 ML)

Eating hot chiles has been shown to actually increase your metabolism, both energizing you and burning more calories. This refreshingly sweet-tart lemonade has just enough of a kick to keep you coming back for more. Start with one jalapeño and see if you want it hotter next time!

Juice the lemon, apples, and jalapeño in that order, or, if using 2 jalapeños, alternate between the apples and jalapeños. Run the pulp through again to extract as much liquid as possible. Serve immediately.

BRAIN BOOSTER

papaya · raspberry · flaxseed · turmeric

5 cups/710 g chopped papaya

1½ cups/170 g raspberries

2 tablespoons flaxseed

One 2-in/5-cm piece fresh turmeric

MAKES ABOUT **2** CUPS

(480 ML)

Anytime you need a little help focusing, buzz up this scarlet drink. Enjoy the sweet and fruity taste, with a little bite from the turmeric. Papaya is rich in antioxidants, while flaxseed adds some essential fatty acids to help your brain work. Fresh turmeric is thought to protect the brain and stop inflammation throughout the body.

Juice the papaya, raspberries, flaxseed, and turmeric, in that order. Run the pulp through again to extract as much liquid as possible. Serve immediately.

PERSIMMON PUNCH

persimmon · pear · cranberry

3 medium persimmons, stemmed

1 ripe medium pear, cored

2 cups/225 g cranberries

MAKES ABOUT 2 CUPS
(480 ML)

Are you a persimmon fan? Or have you never tried one of these mysterious little orange fruits? Persimmons should be allowed to ripen until they are soft and puckered and have turned deep orange to fully develop their deep, sweet flavors. Simply trim the stem end, halve, and drop in the juicer!

Juice the persimmons, pear, and cranberries, in that order. Run the pulp through again to extract as much liquid as possible. Serve immediately.

FRESH AIR

apple · parsley · cucumber

1 large apple, cored

1 cup/30 g packed chopped fresh parsley stems

2 small cucumbers

MAKES ABOUT **2** CUPS

(480 ML)

Use up parsley stems in this juice and enjoy their sprightly flavor with a little soothing cucumber and apple for flavor. Parsley is a famous breath freshener.

Juice the apple, parsley stems, and cucumbers, in that order. Run the pulp through again to extract as much liquid as possible. Serve immediately.

RED RELIEF

strawberry · cherry · celery · apple

1 cup/115 g strawberries,
hulled

1 cup/115 g cherries, pitted

4 celery ribs

1 large apple, cored

MAKES ABOUT **2** CUPS
(480 ML)

Achy joints and tight muscles are often signs of inflammation. Sip this gloriously red juice and flood those pesky pains with cherry and apple polyphenols, known for their anti-inflammatory goodness. Sour cherries are more potent, but sweet cherries are good, too. The juicy berry and cherry flavors beat aspirin any day.

Juice the strawberries, cherries, celery, and apple, in that order. Run the pulp through again to extract as much liquid as possible. Serve immediately.

PINEAPPLE DIGESTIF

pineapple · ginger · papaya

3 cups/455 g pineapple cubes

One 2-in/5-cm piece fresh ginger

2 cups/280 g papaya cubes

MAKES ABOUT **2** CUPS
(480 ML)

The sweet-tart flavors of the pineapple and papaya get a gingery zing, which brightens this creamy concoction. Both pineapple and papaya contain enzymes that aid digestion, and ginger is another great digestive aid, too.

Juice the pineapple, ginger, and papaya, in that order. Run the pulp through again to extract as much liquid as possible. Serve immediately.

MONSOON SEASON

pineapple · turmeric · orange · lemon · cinnamon

2 cups/320 g pineapple cubes
(1 cup/170 g if using a blender)

One 1-in/2.5-cm piece fresh
turmeric

3 large oranges, peeled and
seeded (1 if using a blender)

½ large lemon, peeled and
seeded

¼ teaspoon ground cinnamon

MAKES ABOUT **2** CUPS

(480 ML)

Comfort yourself when the temperature becomes very hot or very cold with this tasty, sweet juice. Pineapple and orange are sweet and tangy, and anti-inflammatory turmeric will soothe your body on the inside. Cinnamon is delicious and has been found to lower blood sugar and help lower cholesterol levels.

For the juicer: Juice the pineapple, turmeric, oranges, lemon, and cinnamon, in that order. Run the pulp through again to extract as much liquid as possible. Serve immediately.

For the blender: Combine the pineapple, turmeric, orange, lemon, and cinnamon in the blender and process until smooth. Serve immediately.

SNIFFLE SQUELCHER

pineapple · kiwi · orange · echinacea tea

3 cups/455 g pineapple chunks
(2 cups/320 g if using a
blender)

2 kiwi, peeled

2 large oranges, peeled

½ cup/120 ml brewed echinacea
tea, chilled

MAKES ABOUT **2** CUPS
(480 ML)

Feel a cold coming on? This sweet-tart cocktail of vitamin C–rich fruits gets an extra boost from echinacea. You can use your juicer for a sippable juice or the blender for a thicker concoction. Just thin to the desired consistency with tea.

For the juicer: Juice the pineapple, kiwi, and oranges, in that order. Run the pulp through again to extract as much liquid as possible. Pour into a glass, add the tea, and stir until combined. Serve immediately.

For the blender: Combine the pineapple, kiwi, oranges, and tea in the blender and process until smooth. Serve immediately.

ANTIOXIDANT POM-PEAR

pomegranate · pear

1 cup/140 g pomegranate seeds (arils)

2 ripe medium pears, cored

½ cup/120 ml sparkling water

MAKES ABOUT **2** CUPS
(480 ML)

This delicious and refreshing pink spritzer is packed with antioxidants. Tart pomegranate seeds give up their scarlet juice and mix with smooth, sweet pears to brighten your day.

Juice the pomegranate seeds and pears, in that order. Pour into a glass, add the sparkling water, and stir until combined. Serve immediately.

03

RELAXING
juices

We live in an age in which life is accelerated. It's very easy to become overwhelmed by pressure and stress. That's why it is so important to take time to relax. Making a juice can be a refreshing ritual. You can stop hurrying toward the future and care for yourself instead.

The juices here are perfect for creating an oasis of calm in your busy day and for nourishing yourself at the same time. Instead of turning to a cookie for comfort, honor yourself by making an elixir of beautiful fruits and veggies.

You can find many unhealthful ways to unwind, but you don't need them. Happy hour becomes really happy when you turn it into a juicing party. Drink a fresh glass of Apple Pie (page 95) with warming cinnamon, and just breathe. Chill out with Watermelon Agua Fresca (page 93) or a Strawberry-Banana Spritzer (page 101). You will never want sugary soda when you develop a taste for real food juices.

Juices can take advantage of the naturally relaxing properties of certain foods. Potassium and magnesium are important minerals for relaxation, and sipping on a Potassium Soother (page 94) or a Mag Melon (page 90) will help take the edge off in the most delightful way. Lettuce has been a sleep aid since Roman times; it contains minute amounts of an opium-like substance. Juicing a few leaves and sipping Sleepy Salad (page 84) may well help you fall asleep.

So kick back, relax, and sip on one of the refreshing juices that follow. Your body will thank you.

CUCUMBER HERBAL

cucumber · parsley · thyme · orange

1 large cucumber

1 cup/30 g packed fresh parsley, leaves and stems

1 tablespoon fresh thyme leaves

2 large oranges, peeled and seeded

MAKES ABOUT **2** CUPS

(480 ML)

Thyme and parsley are both antibacterial, and with cooling cucumber, this drink will salve a sore throat and help fight infection. These greens are also deliciously peppery and herbal, giving your juice a unique savory quality.

Juice the cucumber, parsley, thyme, and oranges, in that order. Run the pulp through again to extract as much liquid as possible. Serve immediately.

IS IT RIPE?

When selecting produce for your juices, you want to get the freshest, ripest fruits and vegetables. This is essential for great flavor and also for nutrition. The fact is, a fully ripened fruit has more vitamins, minerals, and antioxidants than an under-ripe one.

Some fruits are what is called "climacteric," which means that they can be picked while under-ripe and ripened later. Apples, bananas, apricots, peaches, plums, cantaloupes, mangoes, kiwi, pears, persimmons, tomatoes, and avocados all are climacteric fruits. We are all accustomed to buying green bananas and waiting for them to ripen. As a juicer, you can keep a basket of climacteric fruits handy, and juice whatever is ripest. When your favorites are in season, buy them as close to ripe as possible, especially tomatoes. Most apples are already ripe when they arrive in stores, so keep them refrigerated.

Non-climacteric fruits include citrus, pineapples, grapes, and some strawberries. If you see pineapples that have all green skin, they are not ripe and will never ripen. Citrus is usually picked ripe and has a sturdy, padded skin to protect it, but it will dry out if left out, so keep it in the refrigerator.

Vegetables are simpler. Vegetables should be picked fully ripe and rushed to market. Look for firm, unblemished veggies. Leafy greens should never be limp or slimy. Root veggies, like beets and carrots, can be stored for longer periods, but if their skins look thick and rough, or they feel lighter than usual, that is a sign they have been languishing in the produce case.

WALDORF

celery · parsley · walnut · apple

6 **celery ribs**

1½ **cups/45 g packed fresh parsley, leaves and stems**

2 **tablespoons chopped walnuts**

1 **large apple, cored**

MAKES ABOUT **2** CUPS

(480 ML)

The classic Waldorf salad is a pile of apples, celery, walnuts, and mayonnaise, but you can enjoy its flavors in this juice without the mayo getting in the way. Walnuts give the juice a nutty taste as well as a little more bulk to fill you up. They are rich in essential fatty acids and very good for your brain.

Juice the celery, parsley, walnuts (see Note), and apple, in that order. Run the pulp through again to extract as much liquid as possible. Serve immediately.

Note: If your juicer can't handle walnuts, leave them out and juice the other ingredients. Mince the walnuts very finely and then crush them with the side of a chef's knife to make a paste. Transfer to a cup and gradually whisk in a little of the juice. Stir the walnut mixture into the remaining juice until blended.

83

RELAXING
JUICES

SLEEPY SALAD

romaine · dill · cucumber

1 head romaine lettuce

2 tablespoons fresh chopped dill

1 large cucumber

MAKES ABOUT **2** CUPS

(480 ML)

Lettuce has been known for its sleep-inducing properties since Ancient Roman days. The dill gives this deep-green drink a delightful herbal quality and imparts a calming effect. Drink this a couple of hours before bedtime.

Juice the romaine, dill, and cucumber, in that order. Run the pulp through again to extract as much liquid as possible. Serve immediately.

GORGEOUS GRAPEFRUIT AND GREENS

grapefruit · spinach · romaine · cucumber

2 red grapefruit, peeled

2 cups/55 g packed spinach

4 cups/115 g packed romaine
lettuce

1 medium cucumber

MAKES ABOUT **2** CUPS
(480 ML)

Sweet-tart grapefruit gives your greens a kiss of pink while transforming a green juice into a tangy cocktail. Romaine lettuce is a great source of everything leafy greens are famous for, including lots of vitamin A.

Juice the grapefruit, spinach, romaine, and cucumber, in that order. Run the pulp through again to extract as much liquid as possible. Serve immediately.

GRAPE NIGHT'S SLEEP

grape · butter lettuce · chamomile tea

2 cups/250 g purple grapes

3 cups/170 g packed butter lettuce

½ cup/120 ml brewed chamomile tea, chilled

MAKES ABOUT **2** CUPS

(480 ML)

Deep purple grapes give this juice loads of vitamin C, while the mild butter lettuce is a soporific, which can help you fall asleep at night. Chamomile tea has a sweet herbal flavor and helps relax you. Drink this while relaxing in a warm bath an hour before bed.

Juice the grapes and the lettuce, alternating between the two. Pour into a glass, add the cold tea, and stir to combine. Serve immediately.

PINKY MELON

grape · strawberry · watermelon

**2 cups/250 g red grapes
(1 cup/125 g if using a blender)**

**2 cups/225 g strawberries,
hulled (1 cup/115 g if using
a blender)**

**2 cups/290 g seedless
watermelon cubes**

MAKES ABOUT **2** CUPS

(480 ML)

Children, in particular, will love this sweet, pink elixir. The red pigments that make these fruits so colorful are all antioxidants, and the skins of red grapes have the same heart-healthy benefits as wine.

For the juicer: Juice the grapes, strawberries, and watermelon, in that order. Run the pulp through again to extract as much liquid as possible. Serve immediately.

For the blender: Combine the grapes, strawberries, and watermelon in the blender and process until smooth. Serve immediately.

BERRY MELON

cantaloupe · blueberry · raspberry

6 cups/1.2 kg cantaloupe
cubes (2 cups/380 g if using a
blender)

1 cup/170 g blueberries
(½ cup/75 g if using a blender)

1 cup/115 g raspberries
(½ cup/60 g if using a blender)

½ cup/120 ml plain kombucha
(if using a blender)

MAKES ABOUT **2** CUPS

(480 ML)

Go ahead: Buy a huge cantaloupe at the market. You can use it up in this delicious juice, which also makes the most of some antioxidant- and vitamin C–rich berries.

For the juicer: Juice the cantaloupe, blueberries, and raspberries, in that order. Run the pulp through again to extract as much liquid as possible. Serve immediately.

For the blender: Combine the cantaloupe, blueberries, raspberries, and kombucha in the blender and process until smooth. Serve immediately.

MAG MELON

honeydew · spinach · basil

4 cups/570 g honeydew cubes

5 cups/140 g packed spinach

1 cup/60 g packed fresh basil, leaves and stems

MAKES ABOUT **2** CUPS
(480 ML)

Magnesium-rich spinach helps you relax and gives you a good dose of other minerals, as well. Basil adds a lovely herbal flavor and some relaxing, antistress magic. Melon makes this a sweet juice, rich in vitamin C.

Juice the honeydew, spinach, and basil, alternating between the three. Run the pulp through again to extract as much liquid as possible. Serve immediately.

WATERMELON AGUA FRESCA

watermelon · mint

5 cups/800 g seedless watermelon cubes (3 cups/455 g if using a blender)

¾ cup/25 g fresh mint (¼ cup/ 10 g if using a blender)

½ cup/120 ml sparkling water

MAKES ABOUT **2** CUPS
(480 ML)

Watermelon is mostly water, so juicing it is a breeze. The sweet pink drink gets a little more cooling from the addition of mint, which aids digestion and has a calming effect, too.

For the juicer: Juice the watermelon and mint, alternating between the two. Run the pulp through again to extract as much liquid as possible. Pour into a glass, add the sparkling water, and stir to combine. Serve immediately.

For the blender: Combine the watermelon, mint, and sparkling water in the blender and process until smooth. Serve immediately.

POTASSIUM SOOTHER

avocado · banana · orange · kombucha

½ medium avocado, peeled

1 medium banana, peeled

1 large orange, peeled and seeded

1 cup/240 ml plain kombucha

MAKES ABOUT **2** CUPS

(480 ML)

Potassium is calming to the nerves and important to heart health. This smooth purée has a sweet, creamy texture with the pleasing fizz of kombucha. Kombucha is a great way to spritz your drink with added probiotics.

Combine the avocado, banana, orange, and half of the kombucha in the blender and process until smooth. Pour into a glass. Pour the remaining kombucha into the blender and process. Add it to the glass and stir to combine. Serve immediately.

APPLE PIE

apple · cinnamon · vanilla

2 large red apples, cored

2 large green apples, cored

½ teaspoon ground cinnamon

⅛ teaspoon vanilla extract

½ cup/120 ml sparkling water

MAKES ABOUT **2** CUPS
(480 ML)

Don't open another juice box—not when you can make this delicious sweet juice cocktail. Hints of vanilla and cinnamon make it a real dessert in a glass.

Juice the apples and run the pulp through again to extract as much liquid as possible. Pour into a glass and whisk in the cinnamon and vanilla. Add the sparkling water and stir to combine. Serve immediately.

PURPLE HAZE

blueberry · blackberry · grape

1 cup/170 g blueberries

1 cup/145 g blackberries

3 cups/380 g purple or red grapes

MAKES ABOUT **2** CUPS

(480 ML)

Think purple and combine tangy blackberries and blueberries with sweet purple grapes for a decidedly colorful cocktail. Put berries to work fighting pesky free radicals—deliciously.

Juice the blueberries, blackberries, and grapes, in that order. Run the pulp through again twice to extract as much liquid as possible. Serve immediately.

MANGO MELLOW OUT

mango · orange · banana

3 medium mangoes
(1 if using a blender)

2 large oranges, peeled and
seeded (1 if using a blender)

1 medium banana, peeled
(½ banana if using a blender)

Sparkling water
(if using a blender, optional)

MAKES ABOUT **2** CUPS
(480 ML)

Pure tropical flavor will be in your glass when you make this gorgeous sunset-hued beverage. Mangoes are full of relaxing vitamin C as well as healthy digestive enzymes. Bananas boost your potassium.

For the juicer: Juice the mangoes, oranges, and banana, in that order. Run the pulp through again to extract as much liquid as possible. Serve immediately.

For the blender: Combine the mango, orange, and ½ banana in the blender and process until smooth. If you want a thinner drink, add a little sparkling water and blend until smooth. Serve immediately.

PEAR CHAI

pear · lemon · cardamom · clove · cinnamon · chai tea

4 ripe medium pears
(3 if using a blender)

½ large lemon, peeled and
seeded

⅛ teaspoon ground cardamom

⅛ teaspoon ground cloves

⅛ teaspoon ground cinnamon

½ to 1 cup/120 to 240 ml brewed
chai tea, chilled

MAKES ABOUT **2** CUPS
(480 ML)

If you love chai tea, try this fruity version. The spices are all warming in nature, while the smooth pear juice creates an almost creamy backdrop effect.

For the juicer: Juice the pears and lemon, in that order. Whisk in the cardamom, cloves, and cinnamon. Pour into a glass, add ½ cup/120 ml chai tea, and stir until combined. Serve immediately.

For the blender: Combine the pears, lemon, cardamom, cloves, cinnamon, and 1 cup/240 ml chai tea in the blender and process until smooth. Serve immediately.

STRAWBERRY-BANANA SPRITZER

strawberry · banana

2 cups/225 g strawberries, hulled

1 medium banana, peeled

½ cup/120 ml sparkling water or kombucha

MAKES ABOUT **2** CUPS
(480 ML)

If you are looking for a tasty drink that will serve as a snack, too, juice up this beauty. Comforting banana will mellow your mood, and the kombucha will support your healthy digestion.

Juice the strawberries and banana, in that order. Pour into a glass, add the sparkling water, and stir to combine. Serve immediately.

RASPBERRY-APPLE SHRUB

raspberry · apple · apple cider vinegar

1 cup/115 g raspberries

2 large sweet apples, such as Gala or Fuji

2 tablespoons apple cider vinegar

MAKES ABOUT **2** CUPS
(480 ML)

A shrub is an old-fashioned drink, in which vinegar is blended with syrups and extracts of fruits and herbs. This one tastes great, with a bright red raspberry–apple flavor and a kick from apple cider vinegar. The vinegar is one of the original probiotics, long pre-scribed for good health.

Juice the raspberries and apples, in that order. Run the pulp through again to extract as much liquid as possible. Pour into a glass, add the vinegar, and stir to combine. Serve immediately.

04

PURE PLEASURE
juices

Juicing is a great alternative to most beverages, whether you crave sodas or cocktails. With jewel-hued, delicious juice drinks, you can indulge without any regret. With your juicer, you can also make tongue-tingling, alcohol-free juices with the flavors you savor in a cocktail.

If you enjoy the flavors of a mojito, try a Cucumber Mojito (facing page), and sample it alcohol-free. A Chipotle Mary (page 107) adds the smoky flavor of chipotle chile to the familiar tomato cocktail for a peppery kick. The Ginger Piña Colada (page 115) has none of the cloying sweetness of bar versions and lightens up the drink with fresh pineapple and healthy coconut water.

Of course, you can use these delicious juices as mixers, too. Pure, fresh juices make a superior cocktail, with or without alcohol. If you do want an alcoholic drink, you may as well imbibe some vitamins with it. They just might make you feel better the next day.

CUCUMBER MOJITO

cucumber · grape · mint · lime

1 medium cucumber

2 cups/250 g green grapes

¼ cup/10 g packed fresh mint

1 lime, peeled

MAKES ABOUT **2** CUPS

(480 ML)

Go south of the border with this juice, which mimics the mint and lime flavors of the popular cocktail. This one tastes delicious over ice.

Juice the cucumber, grapes, mint, and lime, in that order. Run the pulp through again to extract as much liquid as possible. Serve immediately.

CHIPOTLE MARY

tomato · celery · bell pepper · chipotle

3 medium tomatoes, peeled

3 celery ribs

1 cup/85 g chopped red bell pepper

½ teaspoon ground chipotle chile

MAKES ABOUT **2** CUPS

(480 ML)

Velvety tomatoes spiked with the sweet and smoky flavors of red bell pepper and chipotle will perk you right up. This is a great nonalcoholic aperitif; serve it while you are waiting for dinner, instead of filling up on chips and salsa.

Juice the tomatoes, celery, and bell pepper, alternating between the three. Pour into a glass, add the chipotle, and stir until combined. Serve immediately.

TANGY TOMATO

tomato · cucumber · arugula · lemon

2 large tomatoes, peeled

1 small cucumber

2 cups/55 g packed arugula

½ lemon, peeled and seeded

MAKES ABOUT **2** CUPS

(480 ML)

Sweet and tangy tomatoes, smooth cucumber juice, and the nutty, herbal flavor of arugula make a delightful veggie drink. A spritz of lemon reminds you just how sweet those ripe tomatoes really are.

Juice the tomatoes, cucumber, arugula, and lemon, in that order. Run the pulp through again to extract as much liquid as possible. Serve immediately.

CITRUS PREP

Most of the time, you will want to peel your oranges, grapefruits, lemons, and limes before adding them to the juicer. You can peel by hand or with a knife. If you are comfortable with a chef's knife, you may find it faster and easier. Simply slice off the top and bottom of the fruit to expose the pulp and make a flat, stable bottom, then place the fruit on the cutting board and slice down, following the curve of the fruit, to remove the peel.

Some schools of thought advocate leaving some, or even all, of the peel on the fruit. The white pith, with its bitter flavor, is actually full of anticancer, antioxidant nutrients. The zest that surrounds the pith contains intensely flavorful oils that are also imbued with health-promoting properties.

If you think you'd like to try adding some of the pith and zest to your drink, just do a messy job of peeling and leave a little on the fruit. Juice it and see how it tastes. If it's bitter, by all means, don't think you have to do it again.

Remember, it's only healthful if you drink it, and you won't drink it if you don't like it!

SUPERFRUIT SANGRIA

grape · orange · raspberry

2 cups/250 g red grapes

1 large navel orange, peeled and seeded

1 blood orange, peeled and seeded

1 cup/115 g raspberries

MAKES ABOUT **2** CUPS

(480 ML)

Sangria is a classic way to serve healthy fruit, though in this version I've left out the wine. This is so delicious that you will enjoy all the antioxidants and never miss the alcohol. Serve in a large wine glass, if you like.

Juice the grapes, oranges, and raspberries, in that order. Run the pulp through again to extract as much liquid as possible. Serve immediately.

SUSHI MARTINI

honeydew · cucumber · pear · lemon

2 cups/280 g honeydew cubes

1 medium cucumber

1 ripe medium pear, cored

2 tablespoons fresh lemon juice

MAKES ABOUT **2** CUPS

(480 ML)

Melons are treasured in Japanese cuisine for their delicate flavors and textures. That makes melon a good partner for cukes, which are often included in sushi rolls. For a really elegant drink, serve in a martini glass with an ice cube or two.

Juice the honeydew, cucumber, and pear, in that order. Run the pulp through again to extract as much liquid as possible. Pour into a glass, add the lemon juice, and stir to combine. Serve immediately.

HOLY BASIL MARTINI

mango · basil · coconut water

1½ cups/255 g chopped mango

¼ cup/15 g packed fresh
holy basil, leaves and stems

1 cup/240 ml coconut water

Crushed ice for serving

MAKES ABOUT **2** CUPS
(480 ML)

Looking for a special drink to serve with Thai food? Holy basil has a hint of anise, which you will recognize from your favorite Thai curries. It is used to relieve stress. If you can't find holy basil, use regular basil—both of them provide vitamin A and omega-3 fatty acids.

Combine the mango, basil, and coconut water in the blender and process until smooth. Fill a glass with crushed ice and pour in the juice. Serve immediately.

GINGER PIÑA COLADA

pineapple · ginger · coconut water

2 cups/320 g pineapple cubes

One 1-in/2.5-cm piece fresh ginger

½ cup/120 ml coconut water

MAKES ABOUT **2** CUPS

(480 ML)

Piña coladas are usually made with tons of sugar and booze, but this one is light and lean. Sweet pineapple and electrolyte-rich coconut water get a jolt from fresh ginger, giving you all the buzz you need.

Combine the pineapple, ginger, and coconut water in the blender and process until smooth. Serve immediately.

COSMIC COSMO

pomegranate · apple · pear

¾ cup/100 g pomegranate seeds (arils)

1 large sweet apple, such as Gala or Fuji, seeded

2 ripe medium pears, cored

½ cup/120 ml sparkling water

MAKES ABOUT **2** CUPS
(480 ML)

Put this in a jumbo martini glass and you'll feel pretty cosmopolitan yourself, glamming it up with your pink drink. It's completely healthful, too, with all the antioxidant cred of pomegranate, and the sparkling water gives it fizz.

Juice the pomegranate seeds, apple, and pears, in that order. Pour into a glass, add the sparkling water, and stir to combine. Serve immediately.

BLUE LEMONADE

blueberry · grape · lemon · kombucha

1 cup/170 g blueberries

1½ cups/190 g purple grapes

3 to 4 tablespoons fresh
lemon juice

½ cup/120 ml plain kombucha or
sparkling water

Crushed ice for serving

MAKES ABOUT **2** CUPS
(480 ML)

A classic lemonade is great, but blueberry lemonade is even better. Surprise your guests with a gorgeous purple cocktail over ice, naturally sweetened with grapes and berries.

Combine the blueberries, grapes, lemon juice, and kombucha in the blender and process until smooth. Pour over crushed ice. Serve immediately.

STRAWBERRY-VANILLA SPRITZER

strawberry · apple · vanilla

2 cups/225 g strawberries, hulled

1 large apple, cored

¼ teaspoon vanilla extract

½ cup/120 ml sparkling water

MAKES ABOUT **2** CUPS

(480 ML)

The blend of apple juice with sweet berries and a hint of vanilla makes a delicious drink. The sparkling water is refreshing and adds a little tingle.

Juice the strawberries and apple, in that order. Pour into a glass, add the vanilla and sparkling water, and stir until combined. Serve immediately.

STRAWBERRY DAIQUIRI

strawberry · lime

2 cups/225 g strawberries, hulled

2 tablespoons fresh lime juice

1 cup/240 ml sparkling water

1 tablespoon agave nectar

Crushed ice for serving (optional)

MAKES ABOUT **2** CUPS

(480 ML)

Fresh berries with a twist of lime are so much better than the syrupy daiquiris served in many restaurants. A dab of agave is a great way to sweeten without using sugar.

Combine the strawberries, lime juice, sparkling water, and agave nectar in the blender and process until smooth. Serve over crushed ice, if desired.

PRODUCE MEASUREMENT CONVERSIONS

The sizes and weights of vegetables and fruits vary widely, but fortunately, when it comes to juicing, that doesn't matter very much. The recipes are very forgiving, and even if you use a small apple instead of a large, or 4 carrots instead of 5, the resulting juice will taste delicious. The chart below provides volume and weight equivalents for some of the fruits, vegetables, and herbs in this book. Just remember, the number of flavor combinations you can create is limited only by your imagination (and not strictly by measurements). So use this as a guide to get started, and then experiment.

PRODUCE		OUNCES	CUPS	METRIC
Alfalfa sprouts		2½ oz	2½ cups, packed	70 g
Apple	1 large	9¼ oz		260 g
Arugula		2 oz	2 cups, packed	55 g
Basil, fresh, leaves and stems		1 oz	½ cup, packed	30 g
Beet	1 large	10 oz		280 g
Bell pepper, red, seeded	¼ medium	1½ oz	½ cup, chopped	40 g
	½ medium	3 oz	1 cup, chopped	85 g
	¾ medium	4½ oz	1½ cups, chopped	130 g
	1 medium	6 oz	2 cups, chopped	170 g
Blackberries		5 oz	1 cup	140 g
Blueberries		6 oz	1 cup	170 g

PRODUCE		OUNCES	CUPS	METRIC
Broccoli		4 oz	2 cups, chopped	115 g
Butter lettuce		6 oz	3 cups, packed	170 g
Cabbage, green		2 oz	1 cup, chopped	55 g
Cantaloupe		40 oz	6 cups, cubed	1.2 kg
Carrots	2 medium	4 oz	4 cups, chopped	115 g
	5 medium	9 oz	3 cups, chopped	255 g
	6 medium	12 oz	2 cups, chopped	340 g
	8 medium	16 oz	1 cup, chopped	455 g
Celery	2 ribs	2 oz		55 g
	4 ribs	4 oz		115 g
	8 ribs	8 oz		225 g
	10 ribs	10 oz		280 g
	11 ribs	11 oz		310 g
Chard, red Swiss, leaves and stems	1 leaf	1 oz		30 g
	3 leaves	3 oz		85 g
Cherries, pitted		4 oz	1 cup	115 g
Cilantro, fresh, leaves and stems		½ oz	½ cup, packed	15 g
Collard greens	1 leaf	2 oz	1¼ cups, packed	55 g
	4 leaves	6 oz	4 cups, packed	170 g
	5 leaves	8 oz	5 cups, packed	225 g
Cranberries		6 oz	2 cups	225 g
		8 oz	1½ cups	170 g
Cucumber	1 medium	10 oz		280 g
	1 large	12 oz		340 g
Ginger, fresh	2-in piece	1½ oz		40 g
	1-in piece	¾ oz		20 g
Grapefruit, peeled and seeded	1 small	9 oz		255 g

PRODUCE		OUNCES	CUPS	METRIC
Grapes, green, red, or purple		2½ oz	½ cup	65 g
		4¼ oz	1 cup	125 g
		6¾ oz	1½ cups	190 g
		8¾ oz	2 cups	250 g
		11 oz	2½ cups	315 g
		13½ oz	3 cups	380 g
Honeydew	⅛ melon	10 oz	2 cups, cubed	280 g
	¼ melon	20 oz	4 cups, cubed	570 g
Jalapeño chile	1 medium	½ oz		15 g
Kale, leaves and stems	1 big bunch	7 oz	4 cups, packed	200 g
	1½ big bunches	12 oz	6 cups, packed	340 g
Kiwi, peeled	1 kiwi	2¾ oz		75 g
Mango, pitted and peeled	1 medium	8 oz	2 cups, chopped	225 g
	1½ medium	12 oz	3 cups, chopped	335 g
	2 medium	16 oz	4 cups, chopped	450 g
	2½ medium	20 oz	5 cups, chopped	560 g
Mint, fresh		¼ oz	¼ cup, packed	10 g
		¾ oz	¾ cup, packed	25 g
Papaya	½ medium	10 oz	2 cups, chopped	280 g
	1 large	24 oz	5 cups, chopped	710 g
Parsley, fresh, leaves and stems		¾ oz	¾ cup, packed	20 g
		1 oz	1 cup, packed	30 g
Pear	1 medium	7 oz		200 g
Pea shoots		1½ oz	2 cups	40 g
Persimmon, pitted	1 medium	4 oz		115 g
	3 medium	12 oz		340 g
Pineapple		6 oz	1 cup, cubed	170 g
		11¼ oz	2 cups, cubed	320 g
		16 oz	3 cups, cubed	455 g

PRODUCE		OUNCES	CUPS	METRIC
Plum, pitted	1 medium	2½ oz		70 g
Pomegranate seeds (arils)	1 large pomegranate	5 oz	1 cup	140 g
Radish	2 medium	⅓ oz		10 g
Raspberries		4 oz	1 cup	115 g
		6 oz	1½ cups	170 g
Romaine lettuce	¼ large head	4 oz	4 cups, chopped and packed	115 g
	½ large head	8 oz		225 g
	1 large head	16 oz	8 cups, chopped and packed	455 g
			16 cups, chopped and packed	
Snap peas		6 oz	2 cups	170 g
Spinach, leaves and stems		1 oz	1 cup, packed	30 g
		2 oz	2 cups, packed	55 g
		4 oz	4 cups, packed	115 g
		5 oz	5 cups, packed	140 g
Strawberries, hulled		4 oz	1 cup	115 g
		8 oz	2 cups	225 g
Tomato, plum (Roma), peeled	1 large	4¼ oz		120 g
	2 large	8¾ oz		250 g
	3 large	14¼ oz		375 g
	4 large	16 oz		455 g
	5 large	24 oz		680 g
	6 large	28 oz		800 g
Watercress, leaves and stems		¾ oz	1 cup, packed	20 g
Watermelon, seedless		10¼ oz	2 cups, cubed	290 g
		28 oz	5 cups, cubed	800 g

127

INDEX

130

131

132